The Faith Factor

THE FAITH FACTOR

123 Inspirational Thoughts on Faith

Compiled by
S. Richard Nelson

The Faith Factor

First Edition published 2016

ISBN-13: 978-09904973-1-8
ISBN-10: 0990497313
BISAC: Religion / Christian Life / Spiritual Growth

Artistic Design by Connie Gorton

Broken Hill Publications
Glenwood Springs, CO 81601

"From this broken hill,
All your praises they shall ring."
Leonard Cohen – *If It Be Your Will*

www.srnelson.com

"God is my strength and my power: and he maketh my way perfect."

2 Samuel 22:53

The Faith Factor

Table of Contents

The Faith Factor

Faith

Faith is a grand cathedral, with divinely pictured windows - standing without, you can see no glory, nor can imagine any, but standing within every ray of light reveals a harmony of unspeakable splendors.

- Nathaniel Hawthorne

Let faith be the bridge you build to overcome evil and welcome good.

- Maya Angelou

The Faith Factor

If one has faith one has everything.

- Ramakrishna

Ultimately, blind faith is only kind.

- Mason Cooley

Sometimes your only available transportation is a leap of faith.

- Margaret Shepard

Faith is better measured in terms of quality than of quantity.

- Rich Nelson

Faith is the bridge between where I am and the place God is taking me.

Without faith, hope and trust, there is no promise for the future, and without a promising future, life has no direction, no meaning and no justification.

- Adlin Sinclair

True faith is doing what no one else is doing and traveling the road no one else travels.

All Christians should take every opportunity to develop faith, both in their own lives and in the lives of others. As Christians, faith is our heritage.

- Rich Nelson

Prayer is the key to heaven but faith unlocks the door.

Faith must clearly be at the center of all that we do.

- Rich Nelson

Faith is a bird that feels dawn breaking and sings while it is still dark.

- Rabindranath Tagore

Faith is an oasis in the heart which will never be reached by the caravan of thinking,

- Khalil Gibran

The Faith Factor

Faith, Doubt, Worry & Fear

Without faith a man can do nothing; with it all things are possible.

- Sir William Osler

I would rather err on the side of faith than on the side of doubt.

- Robert Schuler

The Faith Factor

All I have seen teaches me to trust the Creator for all I have not seen.

- Ralph Waldo Emerson

There is nothing that wastes the body like worry, and one who has any faith in God should be ashamed to worry about anything whatsoever.

- Mahatma Gandhi

Faith is believing without seeing, knowing without proof, and sharing without regret.

- Catherine Pulsifer

To one who has faith, no explanation is necessary. To one without faith, no explanation is possible.

- St. Thomas Aquinas

Faith is no irresponsible shot in the dark. It is a responsible trust in God, who knows the desires of your hearts, the dreams you are given, and the goals you have set. He will guide your paths right.

- Robert Schuler

Sorrow looks back, worry looks around, faith looks up.

Faith is like a radar that sees through the fog.

- Corrie Ten Boom

The antidote to frustration is a calm faith, not in your own cleverness, or in hard toil, but in God's guidance.

- Norman Vincent Peale

Fear ends where faith begins.

- Georgio A. Dino

Faith is regarded as the conviction of an unseen God that is even more enduring than the things we see and touch.

- Rich Nelson

Every philosophy is ultimately based upon assumptions which cannot be proven and therefore must be taken by faith.

- Philip L. Troyer

Faith is seeing light with your heart when all your eyes see is darkness.

Faith is the only thing I know that is greater than fear.

- Joyce Meyer

Faith is taking the first step, even when you can't see the whole staircase.

- Martin Luther King, Jr.

Let your faith be bigger than your fears.

Worry ends when faith in God begins.

Feed your faith and your doubts will starve to death.

At the point where hope would otherwise become hopelessness, it becomes faith.

- Robert Brault

Faith and fear both demand that you believe in something you cannot see. You Choose.

- Bob Proctor

Let your dreams be bigger than your fears, your actions louder than your words and your faith stronger than your feelings.

Faith & Knowledge

No living, knowledgeable person, whether serving God or not, acts without faith. You might as well try to live without breathing as to live without the principle of faith.

– Rich Nelson

Faith is not hoping God can. It is knowing He will.

The Faith Factor

Faith is reason grown courageous.

- Sherwood Eddy

Faith is a knowledge within the heart, beyond the reach of proof.

- Khalil Gibran

Faith bridges the gap in the absence of concrete corroboration.

- Rich Nelson

True faith, not head knowledge, is a firm conviction that brings personal surrender to God and His Word.

- Kay Arthur

Faith is not knowing what the future holds, but knowing who holds the future.

We are dependent on our faith for all our knowledge, insight, and intellect. We would never have sought wisdom and intelligence unless we believed that we could acquire them.

- Rich Nelson

Christian faith is logical, rational, and based upon solid historical data, and the information is available to all regardless of age, education, or financial status.

- Dr. A.G. Walp

Spiritual *belief* precedes spiritual *knowledge*. When we believe in things that are not seen but are true, then we have faith.

- Rich Nelson

Faith is evidence! It is the assertion of facts that are otherwise not evident and cannot be proven. Faith in God and Jesus Christ leads us to the knowledge of their existence and divine nature.

- Rich Nelson

Faith is not the same as knowledge; faith must center on something that is *not* known. It must go beyond established evidence, it must venture into the unknown, and it must traverse the edge of light and step into the darkness. If we demand to know everything, if we require that everything be explained, if we insist that everything has to be quantified, then we have no need for faith.

- Rich Nelson

Faith requires that I must first believe that God is (see Heb. 11: 6) - not just believe that God exists, but that He really is fully present whenever and wherever we gather together.

- Ron Larson

Truth is not necessarily found in factual evidence. The lack of proof in the existence of God does not prove that He does not exist.

- Rich Nelson

The Faith Factor

Faith & Power

Faith allows things to happen. It is the power that comes from a fearless heart. And when a fearless heart believes, miracles happen.

Optimism is the faith that leads to achievement. Nothing can be done without hope and confidence.

- Helen Keller

Faith is like WI-FI, it's invisible but it has the power to connect you to what you need.

The Faith Factor

Faith is power. It is a mystical, divine power that surpasses all we can possibly envision.

– Rich Nelson

Faith is daring the soul to go beyond what the eyes can see.

- William Newton Clark

We will not naturally drift into becoming faithful disciples, husbands, and fathers. We must be intentional!

- Jerrad Lopes

It's not what you say that reveals what you truly believe; it's what you do. The Bible says that faith without works is dead.

- James Robor

The only power we have is to turn to God for help, whether we have a lot of faith or not.

- Laurie Penner

Faith with action combined with the glory will get you into the realm of creative miracles faster than anything else - even if you don't understand it.

- David Herzog

Faith is the prevailing principle of power. In fact, without faith there is no power!

- Rich Nelson

It is in our weakness that God wants us to lean on Him so that He can empower us to walk by faith into the divine destiny over our lives.

- E'yen A. Gardner

Faith in the Lord Jesus Christ is an eternal, endless power as great as any power in the whole universe.

- Rich Nelson

Instead of being narrow and dismal, faith is the biggest and brightest thing that can come into your life, transforming every power and inspiring every energy, bathing it in peace and flooding it with joy.

- Brad Hanson

Faith is a principle of action and of power, and by it the faithful Christian can influence any number of circumstances when the occasion warrants.

- Rich Nelson

It is in the act of offering our hearts in faith that something in us transforms...proclaiming that we no longer stand on the sidelines but are leaping directly into the center of our lives, our truth, our full potential.

- Sharon Salzberg

The Faith Factor

The most straightforward description of faith that I have ever seen is "faith is power."

- Rich Nelson

Faith is the strength by which a shattered world shall emerge into the light.

- Helen Keller

No faith is required to do the possible; actually, only a morsel of this atom-powered stuff is needed to do the impossible, for a piece as large as a mustard seed will do more than we have ever dreamed of.

- Leonard Ravenhill

Faith is the force of life.

- Leo Tolstoy

As believing Christians there is a substantial, higher power available to us. It is the power of faith.

– Rich Nelson

Faith can move mountains but don't be surprised if God hands you a shovel.

Faith does not operate in the realm of the possible. There is no glory for God in that which is humanly possible. Faith begins where man's power ends.

- George Mueller

The Faith Factor

Faith & Miracles

Faith is more important to me than life itself because without it there would be no fullness of life.

- Mother Teresa

If we build on our faith and grow spiritually we will see its fruits not only in our lives but when we reach heaven as well.

- Jason A. Ponzio

The Faith Factor

Faith expects from God what is beyond all expectation.

- Andrew Murray

Faith is to believe what we do not see, and the reward of this faith is to see what we believe.

- Augustine

Surrender to what is. Let go of what was. Have faith in what will be.

- Sonia Ricotti

Where there is hope, there is faith. Where there is faith, miracles happen.

Faith sees the invisible, believes the unbelievable and receives the impossible.

- Corrie Ten Boom

If you are submissive, humble, and patient, the Lord will give you everything that is best for you.

- Rich Nelson

Faith doesn't make sense, that's why it makes miracles.

- John Di Lemme

Back of every creation, supporting it like an arch, is faith. Enthusiasm is nothing: It comes and goes. But if one believes, then miracles occur.

- Henry Miller

Today is a day of miracles. Believe in miracles. Expect miracles according to your faith.

- Rich Nelson

We receive all of our earthly blessings by faith and likewise we receive all our spiritual blessings by faith.

- Rich Nelson

A little faith will bring your soul to heaven, A lot of faith will bring heaven to your soul.

- Dwight L. Moody

Is it possible that the smallness of our faith limits God?

- Al Bryant

The Faith Factor

Faith in God & Christ

Faith isn't the ability to believe long and far into the misty future. It's simply taking God at His Word and taking the next step.

- Joni Erickson Tada

Jesus will unlock the treasure house of blessings to anyone who is full of faith.

- Rich Nelson

The Faith Factor

We have a choice of focusing on our problems or focusing on God, who holds the solution.

- Rick Warren

God demands nothing except your faith in Him.

- Elizabeth Edwards

The central precept of any Christian is faith in the Lord Jesus Christ. Faith in Him is basic to peace of mind in this life and hopefulness in the world to come.

- Rich Nelson

Righteousness from God comes through faith in Jesus Christ to all who believe.

- Kim Trujillo

Faith is confidence in the veracity of what God has said.

Resilient, sustainable faith means we choose Christ and his gospel over everything else.

- Rich Nelson

Faith involves believing in a God who loves you so much that he will always do the very best for you.

- Margaret Weston

Faith in the Lord Jesus Christ is fully sustaining. You can cause things to happen by disciplining yourself and paying the price. Be truly committed, and you will see the mountains move in your behalf. "All things are possible to him who believes." (Mark 9:23)

- Rich Nelson

Faith in God helps you foster a personal love for Him, one that is reciprocated by Him through blessing you in your greatest times of need.

- Rich Nelson

So the first step to having massive faith is that we must have accurate faith. Our faith must be in the will of God, and in order for it to be in His will, we must become better listeners.

- Adam Houge

Let your faith be in The Word of God brought by the Spirit of God rather than being in your church, your pastor, or other people.

- Joan Boney

Faith in Jesus Christ is more than simply a pronouncement of belief. Faith in Him entails absolute dependence on Him.

- Rich Nelson

Faith is not the belief that God will do what you want. It is the belief that God will do what is right.

The Faith Factor

Sustainable and resilient faith requires living our lives, day-by-day, as Jesus wants us to live them.

- Rich Nelson

Faith is the gaze of a soul upon a saving God.

- A. W. Tozer

Have faith in God; God has faith in you.

- Edwin Loius Cole

We show resilient faith through firmness, dependability, and stability in the cause of Christ. We display resilient faith when we surrender to Jesus, when we do what he has lovingly invited us to do and cast our burdens at his feet.

- Rich Nelson

Faith & Trials

Faith is deliberate confidence in the character of God whose ways you may not understand at the time.

- Oswald Chambers

The true challenge, as human beings with all our foibles, is to handle these obstacles without losing faith, trusting that our Source will provide for our needs.

- Ace McCloud

The Faith Factor

God is always with us and will bring us through every calamity and hardship if (and this is the key word) we remain faithful and process these difficulties correctly.

- Erol Woods

Let the spirit rise within and be aligned with God and remain steadfast in your faith even through the season of difficulty.

- Carol Nkambule

Difficulties and obstacles are God's challenges to faith. When hindrances confront us in the path of duty, we are to recognize them as vessels for faith to fill with the fullness and all-sufficiency of Jesus.

- A. B. Simpson

Faith makes things possible...not easy.

Resilient, sustainable faith means that when we are in the middle of a personal crisis, financial frustration, unemployment, depression or spiritual drought, we refuse to succumb to our tragic circumstances but allow Jesus, instead, to do the caring, the struggling and the worrying for us.

- Rich Nelson

Faith is what makes life bearable, with all its tragedies and ambiguities and sudden, startling joys.

- Madeleine L'Engle

Be faithful in small things because it is in them that our strength lies.

- Mother Teresa

Resolution is found through faith. It is found through definite and explicit faith in Christ.

- Rich Nelson

As our faith becomes more resilient, we can respond more maturely to trials, temptations and the tragic events that will certainly surface in our lives.

- Rich Nelson

Faith is not simply a patience which passively suffers until the storm is past. Rather, it is a spirit which bears things...with blazing serene hope.

- Corazon Aquino

Faith is the art of holding on to things in spite of your changing moods and circumstances.

- C. S. Lewis

If we desire our faith to be strengthened, we must not shrink from opportunities where our faith may be tried, and therefore, through trial, be strengthened.

- George Mueller

The Faith Factor

Faith is not about everything turning out okay. Faith is about being okay no matter how things turn out.

In order to increase our faith, we must engage in events that cause us to stretch, and we must pray that we will be able to accomplish God's will in these tasks we have set for ourselves.

- Rich Nelson

Keep the faith. The most amazing things in life tend to happen right at the moment you are about to give up hope.

Sometimes life hits you in the head with a brick. Don't lose faith.

- Steve Jobs

123 Inspirational Thoughts on Faith

If you enjoyed this little booklet,

please leave an honest review.

May God bless you

according to your faith.

About S. Richard Nelson

S. Richard Nelson is the author of a variety of published articles on topics such as religious education, family values, health, and politics. His work has appeared in *Christian Education Today, Church Teacher, Parish Teacher, Living with Teenagers, Liberty Magazine,* and many others.

Contact Information:

Broken Hill Publications
Glenwood Springs, CO 91601

Email S. Richard Nelson at: rich@srnelson.com

Visit S. Richard Nelson at: www.srnelson.com

The Faith Factor

Other Books by S. Richard Nelson

Turning Faith into Power
Book 1 of The Powerful Christian Series.

Turning Faith into Power is the first in a series of instructive and inspirational books from The Powerful Christian Series by S. Richard Nelson. The Savior says in Matthew 17:19-20, "For most assuredly I tell you, If you have faith as a grain of mustard seed, you will tell this mountain, move from here to there, and it will move; and nothing will be impossible to you."

What mountains would you remove from your life if you had the faith of a mustard seed?

What's stopping you from removing the obstacles in your life?

Do you utilize your faith as a principle of action and power?

Is your faith centered where it will be most effective?

Do you have adequate faith in yourself?

As believing Christians there is substantial power available to us. It is the power of faith. Through the bounteous mercy and love of Jesus Christ we receive his grace - a divine means of strength. The power available to us through Jesus Christ is very real.

Gaining Power through Prayer
Book 2 in The Powerful Christian Series

Sincere prayer is a fountain of divine power flowing into our lives. Through prayer we gain clear and precise direction. Through prayer we access the strength of character to perform God's will – to do what is right. Prayer is the process we use to place ourselves in contact with God.

The impressive power of prayer warrants the consideration not only of Christians, but of all societies. This little booklet highlights the principle applications and purposes of prayer. It confirms that God does answer our prayers and demonstrates how we can be more aware of those divine answers. It also examines the challenging question of why, at times, it appears that God does not answer us and what we can do about it.

The Added Power of Obedience
Book 3 in The Powerful Christian Series

Two opposing powers grapple in every human heart and our decisions are usually influenced by them, either to do good or to do evil. The spirit of truth will always persuade us to obey God. We all want happiness. We hope for it, live for it, and make it our primary goal in life. But do we live in a way that allows us to enjoy the happiness we desire so deeply?

The way to be happy is simply to believe in Jesus Christ and obey the gospel. When we obey God's law, then we can expect to find the happiness we desire. Obedience to God is not an inconvenience, it is our ultimate aspiration; it is not a stumbling block, it is a powerful and profitable building block.

Sustainable Spirituality
Maintaining Faith in the Face of Adversity

All of us will, in one form or another, experience hardship and misfortune. The common plight of humanity is the experience of adversity, suffering, sickness, or other difficulties. Life can seem strenuous and unreasonably hard and challenging. Our faith is constantly tried and tested. But the pain we experience, the trials we undertake are never wasted opportunities. They will increase our spiritual education and help us develop patience, faith, fortitude and humility. Life's trials will help us build our characters, purify our hearts, enlarge our souls, and make us kinder and more caring children of God.

The development of sustainable spirituality draws us toward living with compassion so that all people on this planet may be sustained. Sustainable spirituality creates an understanding of the underlying connection between the spiritual practice which provides meaning and purpose in our lives and the rest of humanity. Sustainable spiritual practices offer us a deep inner conviction as well as an encompassing compassion for all of God's other children on Earth.

In this book you will:

- Learn the 3 critical areas of preparation.
- Discover the 3 pillars of spiritual sustainability.
- Realize the difference between religion and spirituality.
- Learn the 5 keys to develop personal sustainability practices.
- Examine 8 spiritual sustainability goals.
- Learn how to remain calm amid the convulsions of the Earth.
- Uncover the foundation for finding world peace.
- Discover how to satisfy spiritual thirst and hunger.
- Learn the keys to becoming an energized Christian.
- Learn the 4 obstacles to realizing pure love.
- Learn the 3 faith-factors that affect your spiritual sustainability.

Sustainable spirituality recognizes a deep bond between the people on this planet and understands that all life is worthy of reverence. It allows us to live healthy, harmonious lives on earth, respecting the inter-connected life of the planet and provides a sense for understanding the fundamental foundation that we are all children of God.

The Faith Factor

Again, if you enjoyed this little booklet,

please leave an honest review.

---

www.ingramcontent.com/pod-product-compliance
Lightning Source LLC
Chambersburg PA
CBHW060719030426
42337CB00017B/2920